Library Resources

What Would You Do with an Encyclopedia?

Susan Kralovansky

Consulting Editor, Diane Craig, M.A./Reading Specialist

A Division of ABDO

ABDO
Publishing Company

visit us at www.abdopublishing.com

Published by ABDO Publishing Company, a division of ABDO, P.O. Box 398166, Minneapolis, Minnesota 55439. Copyright © 2013 by Abdo Consulting Group, Inc. International copyrights reserved in all countries. No part of this book may be reproduced in any form without written permission from the publisher. Super SandCastle™ is a trademark and logo of ABDO Publishing Company.

Printed in the United States of America, North Mankato, Minnesota
102012
082013

 PRINTED ON RECYCLED PAPER

Editor: Liz Salzmann
Content Developer: Nancy Tuminelly
Cover and Interior Design and Production: Kelly Doudna, Mighty Media, Inc.
Photo Credits: Kelly Doudna, Shutterstock

Encyclopædia Britannica and World Book, Inc. hold their respective copyrights

Library of Congress Cataloging-in-Publication Data

Kralovansky, Susan.
 What would you do with an encyclopedia? / Susan Kralovansky.
   p. cm. -- (Library resources)
 ISBN 978-1-61783-607-7
 1. Encyclopedias and dictionaries--Juvenile literature. I. Title.
 031--dc15

                          2012946814

Super SandCastle™ books are created by a team of professional educators, reading specialists, and content developers around five essential components—phonemic awareness, phonics, vocabulary, text comprehension, and fluency—to assist young readers as they develop reading skills and strategies and increase their general knowledge. All books are written, reviewed, and leveled for guided reading, early reading intervention, and Accelerated Reader® programs for use in shared, guided, and independent reading and writing activities to support a balanced approach to literacy instruction.

Contents

What would you do if you had an encyclopedia?

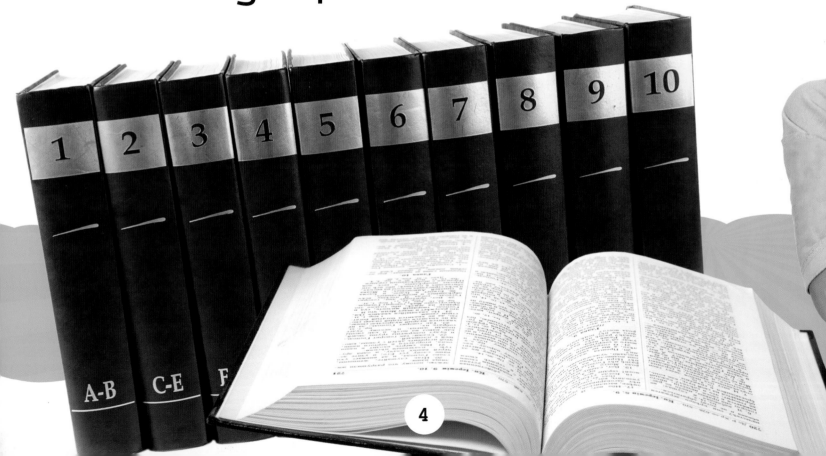

A-B C-E F

An encyclopedia has information about people, places, things, events, and ideas. An encyclopedia helps you learn.

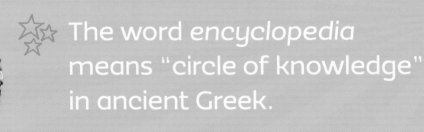

The word *encyclopedia* means "circle of knowledge" in ancient Greek.

6

Encyclopedias come in sets. One encyclopedia set has many books. Each book is called a volume.

set

Britannica

MICROPÆDIA Ready Reference 1 A-ak Bayes

Britannica

MICROPÆDIA Ready Reference 2 Bayeu Ceanothus

Britannica

MICROPÆDIA Ready Reference 3 Ceara Deluc

Britannica

MICROPÆDIA Ready Reference 4 Delusion Frenssen

Britannica

MICROPÆDIA Ready Reference 5 Freon Holderlin

Britannica

MICROPÆDIA Ready Reference 6 Holderness Krasnogorsk

Britannica

MICROPÆDIA Ready Reference 7 Krasnokamsk Menadra

Britannica

MICROPÆDIA Ready Reference 8 Menage Ottawa

Britannica

MICROPÆDIA Ready Reference 9 Otter Rethimnon

Britannica

MICROPÆDIA Ready Reference 10 Reti Solovets

Britannica

MICROPÆDIA Ready Reference 11 Solovyov Truck

Britannica

MICROPÆDIA Ready Reference 12 Trudeau Zywiec

HIST/SOC iDesk

Britannica

MICROPÆDIA
Ready
Reference

1

A-ak
Bayes

HIST/SOC
iDesk

volume

9

Each volume has
a letter on the spine.
Each volume also has
a number on the spine.

volume number

volume letter

2010

1

A

HIST/SOC
Open Ref

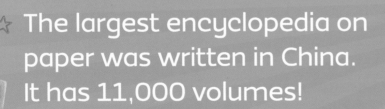

The largest encyclopedia on
paper was written in China.
It has 11,000 volumes!

The **topic** you look up in the encyclopedia is the entry. An entry is the article on your topic.

 Encyclopedias can be general or specific. A specific encyclopedia focuses on a certain topic such as law.

Athens

entry

Athens is the capital of Greece. It is also the largest city in Greece. Athens has a port and two rivers. The city is surrounded by four mountains.

History

People have lived in Athens since at least 7000 BC.

The Odeon of Herodes Atticus on the south slope of the Acropolis in Athens, Greece. The city of Athens is in the background.

Use the index to find out which volume to look in. The index is the last volume in the set.

Index

The index is a list of all the entries in the encyclopedia set. It is in alphabetical order. It tells you the volume and page number where you can find each entry.

The index says that the *Titanic* is in the *T* volume. The *Titanic* entry starts on page 145.

Your topic might also be mentioned in other entries. The index will tell you where to look.

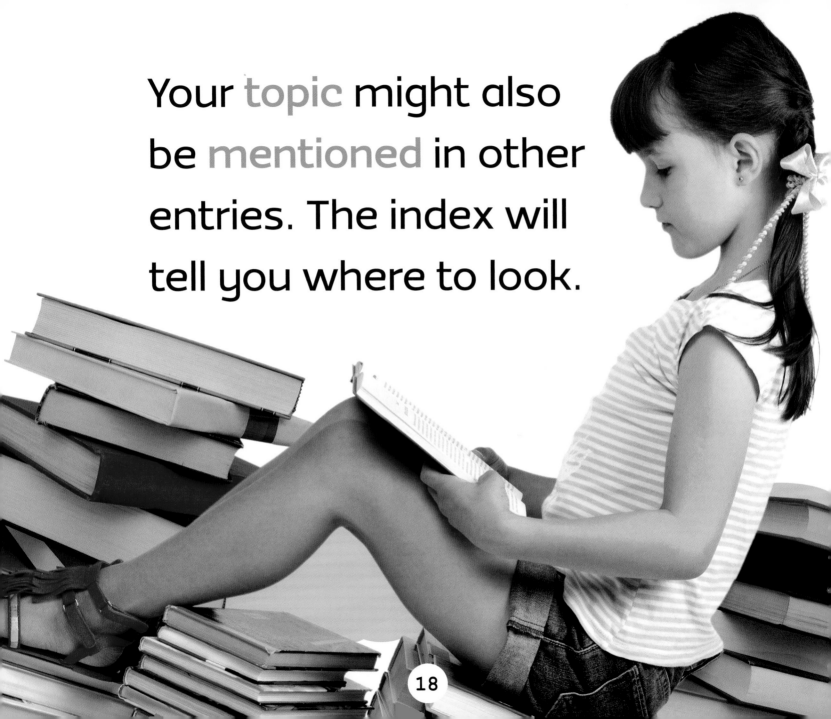

What is an Ice Patrol?

It might lead you to other interesting topics.

Who is David Sarnoff?

Who is David Ballard?

There are two words at the top of every page. They are called guide words. Guide words tell you the first and last entries on the page.

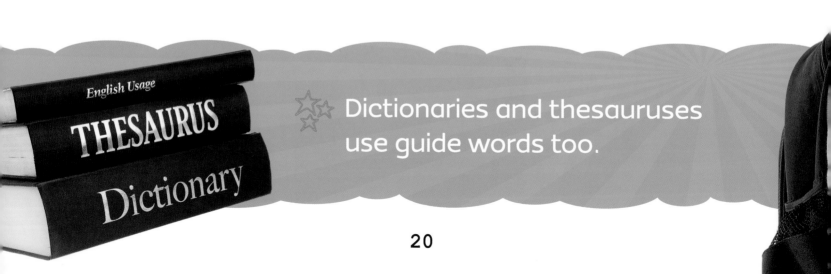

Dictionaries and thesauruses use guide words too.

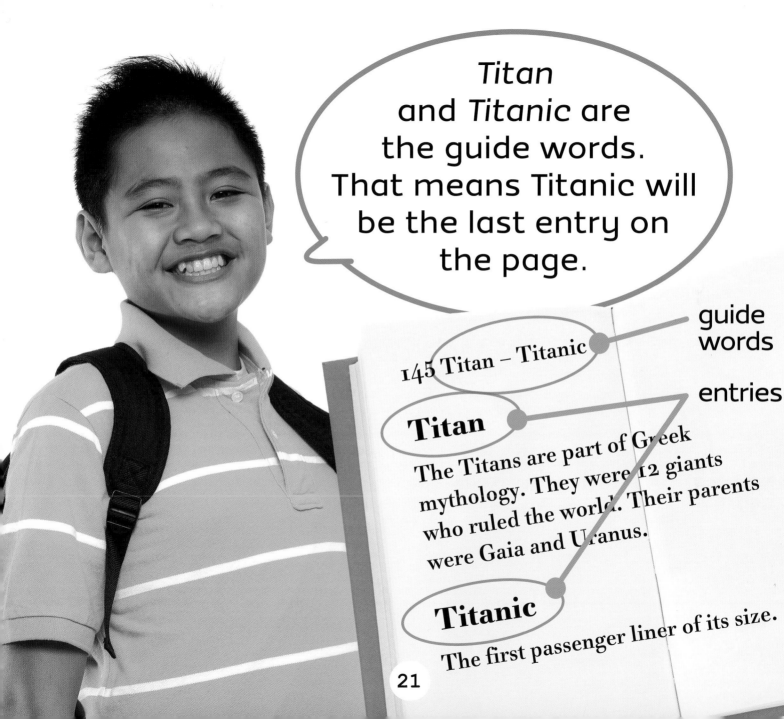

Titan and *Titanic* are the guide words. That means Titanic will be the last entry on the page.

guide words

145 Titan – Titanic

entries

Titan

The Titans are part of Greek mythology. They were 12 giants who ruled the world. Their parents were Gaia and Uranus.

Titanic

The first passenger liner of its size.

Each entry starts with a word in bold print. This is what the entry is about.

The entries in online encyclopedias are in bold type too.

22

entry

Encyclopedia Online
teaching one article at a time

enter sear

home

This article is about the big cat. For other uses, see Tiger (disambiguation).

tiger

CONTENTS
click to jump to section

Overview

Taxonomy and Etymology

Characteristics and Evolution

   Characteristics

   Subspecies

   Extinct Subspecies

Distribution and Habitat

Biology and Behavior

   Territorial Behavior

The tiger has a unique pattern of dark stripes over orange
tiger may be as long as 11 feet and weigh up to 670 pounds
the third largest land carnivore and can live for up to 26 yea

SCIENTIFIC: panthera tigris

REGIONS: Parts of China, India,
North Korea, and Southeast Asia

SIZE: Total body length up to 11 ft (3.3m)
Weight up to 670 lbs (306kg)

A long entry may have several sections. Each section has a heading. The heading tells you what the section is about.

Encyclopedias are everywhere! You can find one at your school or library. There are also online encyclopedias.

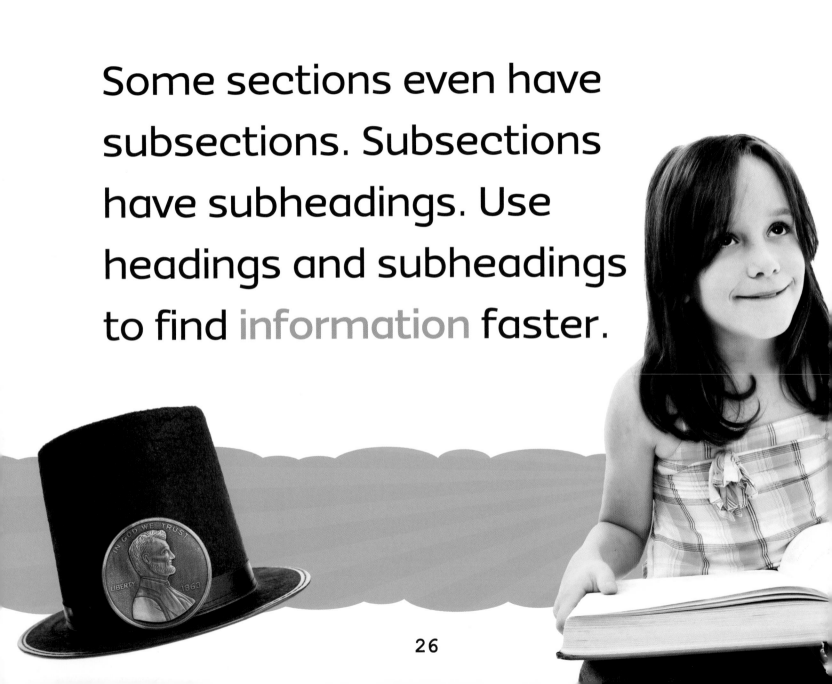

Some sections even have subsections. Subsections have subheadings. Use headings and subheadings to find information faster.

An entry might have pictures, graphs, or maps. They can help you understand the information in the entry.

European Bee-eater

Can reach 10–11.5 inches long. Eats bees, wasps, and hornets. It catches them in mid-air.

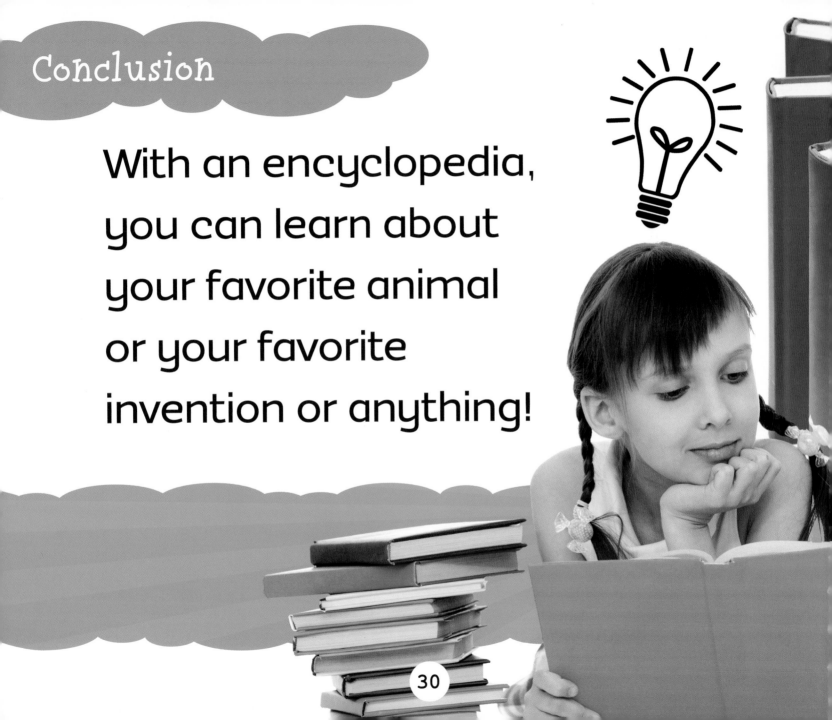

With an encyclopedia, you can learn about your favorite animal or your favorite invention or anything!

Glossary

focus – to concentrate on or pay particular attention to.

graph – a chart or illustration that shows information about the amount of something.

information – something known about an event or subject.

lawyer – a person whose job it is to know the law and to speak for people in court.

mention – to speak about or refer to.

specific – about or related to a certain kind of thing.

spine – the part of a book cover where the pages are attached.

topic – the main idea or subject.